31143011393460
J B Rodgers, A
Scheff, Matt.
Aaron Rodgers /

Main

FOOTBALL'S GREATEST STARS

AARON RODGERS

by Matt Scheff

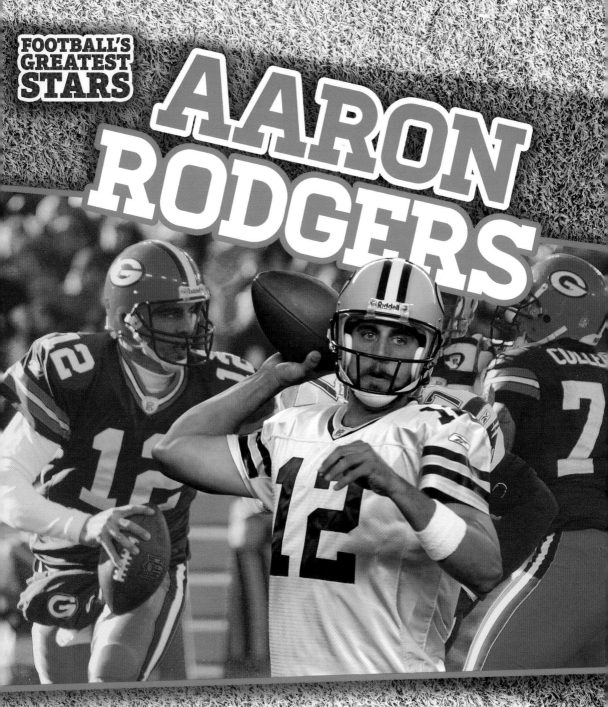

SportsZone

An Imprint of Abdo Publishing
abdopublishing.com

abdopublishing.com

Published by Abdo Publishing, a division of ABDO, PO Box 398166, Minneapolis, Minnesota 55439. Copyright © 2016 by Abdo Consulting Group, Inc. International copyrights reserved in all countries. No part of this book may be reproduced in any form without written permission from the publisher. SportsZone™ is a trademark and logo of Abdo Publishing.

Printed in the United States of America, North Mankato, Minnesota
032015
092015

Cover Photos: Keith Srakocic/AP Images, cover (foreground); Cory Dellenbach/Shawano Leader/AP Images, cover (background)
Interior Photos: Keith Srakocic/AP Images, 1 (foreground); Cory Dellenbach/Shawano Leader/AP Images, 1 (background); Paul Sancya/AP Images, 4-5, 6; Mark Humphrey/AP Images, 7; Kevin Terrell/AP Images, 8-9; Michael Pimentel/Icon Sportswire, 10-11; David Gonzales/Icon Sportswire, 12-13; Dilip Vishwanat/Icon Sportswire, 14-15; Julie Jacobson/ AP Images, 16; Gail Burton/AP Images, 17; LM Otero/AP Images, 18-19; Steve Apps/Wisconsin State Journal/AP Images, 20-21; Charles Rex Arbogast/AP Images, 22-23; Carlos Osorio/AP Images, 24-25; David Stluka/AP Images, 26-27, 28-29

Editor: Nick Rebman
Series Designer: Jake Nordby

Library of Congress Control Number: 2015932401

Cataloging-in-Publication Data
Scheff, Matt.
 Aaron Rodgers / Matt Scheff.
   p. cm. -- (Football's greatest stars)
Includes index.
ISBN 978-1-62403-827-3
1. Rodgers, Aaron, 1983- --Juvenile literature. 2. Football players--United States--Biography--Juvenile literature. 3. Quarterbacks (Football)--United States--Biography--Juvenile literature.   I. Title.
796.332092--dc23
[B]   2015932401

CONTENTS

SUPER BOWL CHAMPION

Quarterback Aaron Rodgers took the snap. The Super Bowl crowd was on its feet. Green Bay Packers wide receiver Jordy Nelson streaked down the sideline. Rodgers lofted a perfect pass over the Pittsburgh Steelers defender. Nelson hauled it in and fell into the end zone. Touchdown! 7-0 Packers!

FAST FACT

In 2011 Rodgers became just the fourth quarterback in National Football League (NFL) history to throw for 300 yards, three touchdowns, and no interceptions in a Super Bowl.

Rodgers throws a pass during the 2011 Super Bowl.

In the second quarter, Rodgers zipped a ball to wide receiver Greg Jennings for a touchdown. Green Bay was up 21-3. But Pittsburgh roared back to make the score 21-17. Rodgers led his team down the field. He fired a pass to Jennings in the back of the end zone. Touchdown! The Packers were on their way to a 31-25 victory.

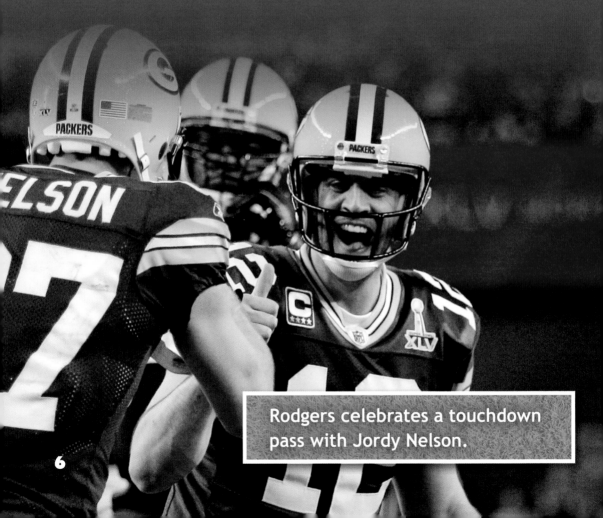

Rodgers celebrates a touchdown pass with Jordy Nelson.

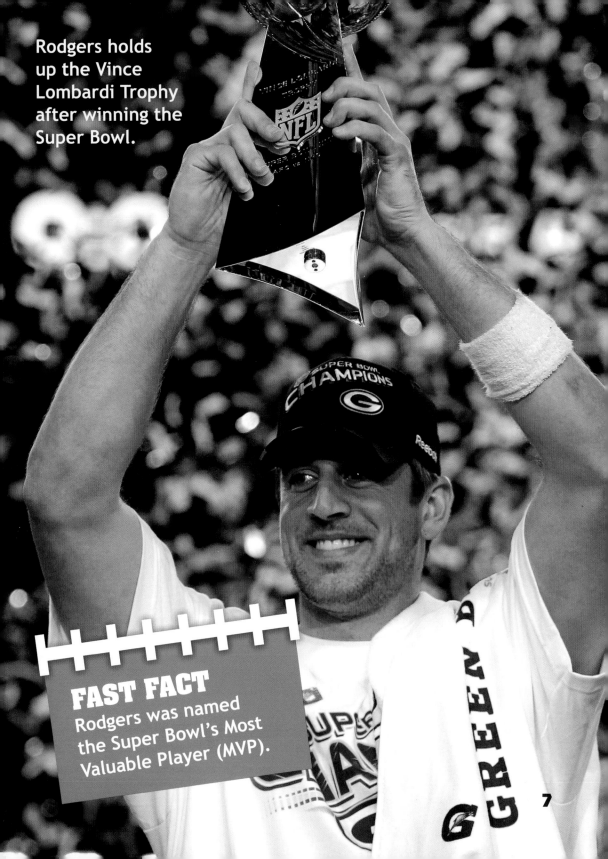

Rodgers holds up the Vince Lombardi Trophy after winning the Super Bowl.

FAST FACT
Rodgers was named the Super Bowl's Most Valuable Player (MVP).

7

EARLY LIFE

Aaron Rodgers was born on December 2, 1983, in Chico, California. As a child, he and his two brothers loved to throw the football with their dad, Ed. Ed Rodgers had played college and semi-pro football as a young man. He passed on his love of the game to all three of his boys.

FAST FACT

As a boy, Aaron loved to watch his favorite NFL player, San Francisco 49ers quarterback Joe Montana.

Rodgers celebrates with his family after winning the Super Bowl.

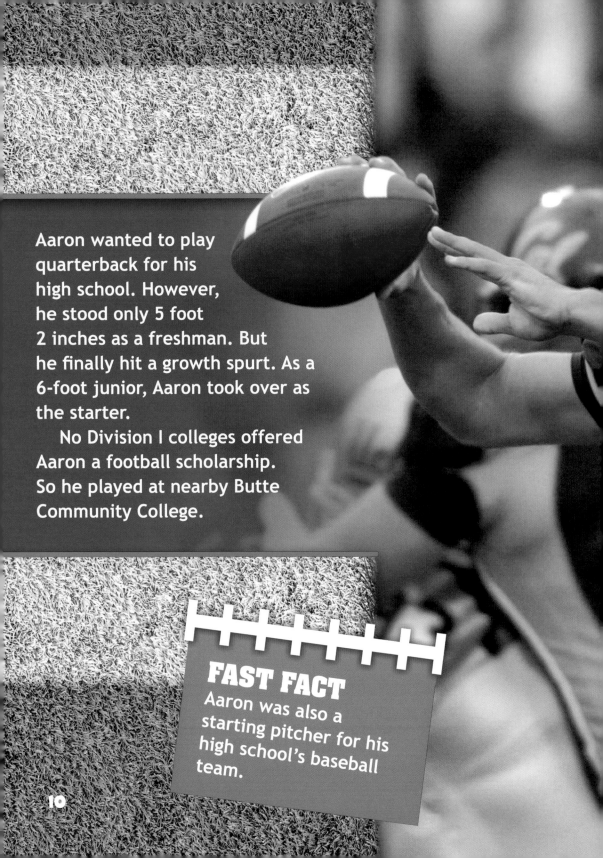

Aaron wanted to play quarterback for his high school. However, he stood only 5 foot 2 inches as a freshman. But he finally hit a growth spurt. As a 6-foot junior, Aaron took over as the starter.

No Division I colleges offered Aaron a football scholarship. So he played at nearby Butte Community College.

FAST FACT

Aaron was also a starting pitcher for his high school's baseball team.

Rodgers passes the ball during a college football game against the University of California, Los Angeles.

COLLEGE MAN

Rodgers started as a freshman for Butte in 2002. Coaches at the University of California, Berkley, came to Butte's games to scout one of Rodgers's teammates. But California coach Jeff Tedford was impressed with the quarterback. He offered Rodgers a scholarship. Rodgers left Butte for California after only one season.

Rodgers leads California to a big win over Stanford.

FAST FACT
Rodgers threw 43 touchdown passes and only 13 interceptions in his two seasons at California.

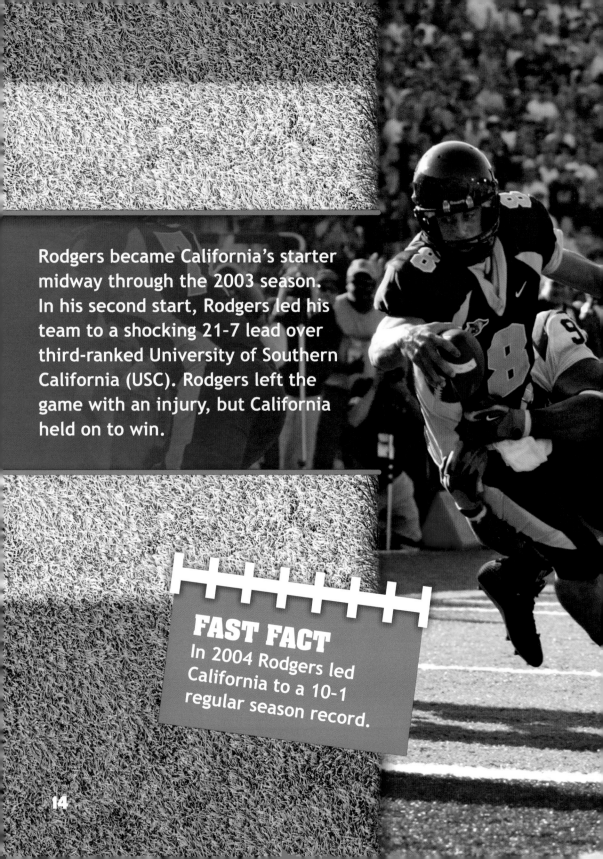

Rodgers became California's starter midway through the 2003 season. In his second start, Rodgers led his team to a shocking 21-7 lead over third-ranked University of Southern California (USC). Rodgers left the game with an injury, but California held on to win.

FAST FACT

In 2004 Rodgers led California to a 10-1 regular season record.

Rodgers scores a touchdown in California's victory against USC.

WELCOME TO THE NFL

Many NFL teams noticed Rodgers's football smarts and athletic ability. So Rodgers left college early and entered the 2005 NFL Draft.

Many experts thought Rodgers could be the top pick. His favorite team, the 49ers, had that selection. But the 49ers chose Utah quarterback Alex Smith. So Rodgers waited. Pick after pick was announced. Finally, the Green Bay Packers chose Rodgers with the twenty-fourth selection.

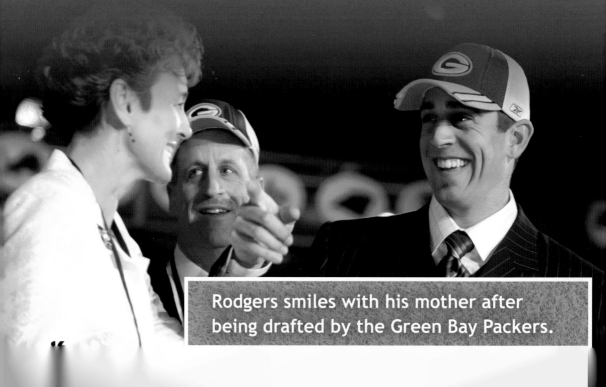

Rodgers smiles with his mother after being drafted by the Green Bay Packers.

Rodgers attempts a pass during his rookie season.

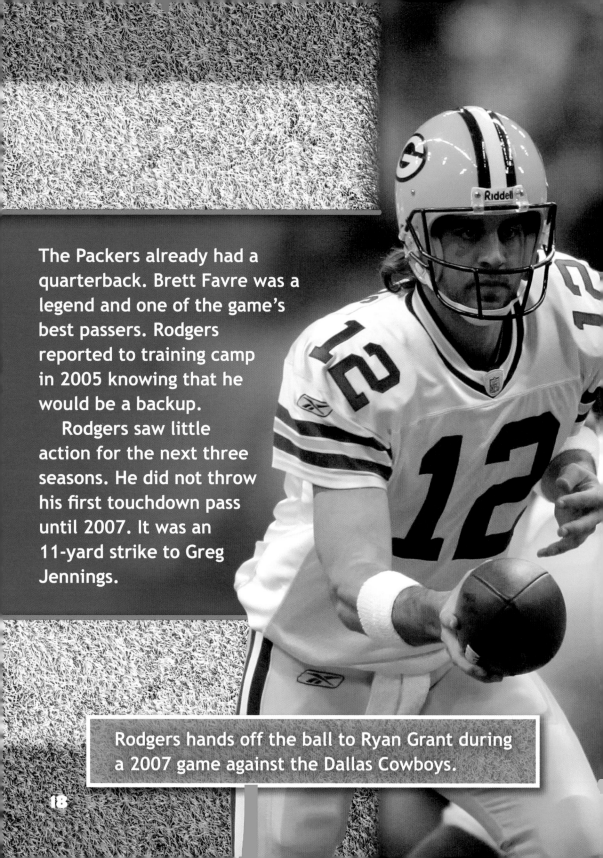

The Packers already had a quarterback. Brett Favre was a legend and one of the game's best passers. Rodgers reported to training camp in 2005 knowing that he would be a backup.

Rodgers saw little action for the next three seasons. He did not throw his first touchdown pass until 2007. It was an 11-yard strike to Greg Jennings.

Rodgers hands off the ball to Ryan Grant during a 2007 game against the Dallas Cowboys.

FAST FACT

Favre led the Packers to a Super Bowl victory in January 1997.

MAKING A MARK

Favre was traded to the New York Jets in 2008. The Packers were ready for Rodgers to take over. Rodgers played well, but the team struggled to a 6-10 record.

Green Bay's fortunes began to turn in 2009. The Packers made the playoffs but lost to the Arizona Cardinals.

Rodgers spikes the ball after scoring a touchdown in his first NFL start.

FAST FACT

The Cardinals beat the Packers 51-45 in their playoff game. It was the highest-scoring playoff game in NFL history.

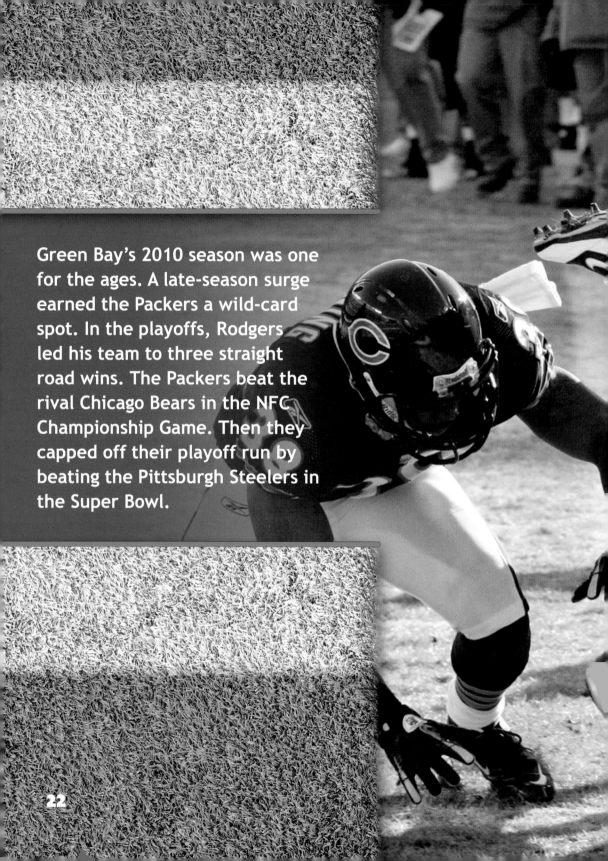

Green Bay's 2010 season was one for the ages. A late-season surge earned the Packers a wild-card spot. In the playoffs, Rodgers led his team to three straight road wins. The Packers beat the rival Chicago Bears in the NFC Championship Game. Then they capped off their playoff run by beating the Pittsburgh Steelers in the Super Bowl.

Rodgers scores a touchdown against the Chicago Bears in the NFC Championship Game.

FAST FACT

The Packers' memorable playoff run included a 48-21 pounding of the top-seeded Atlanta Falcons.

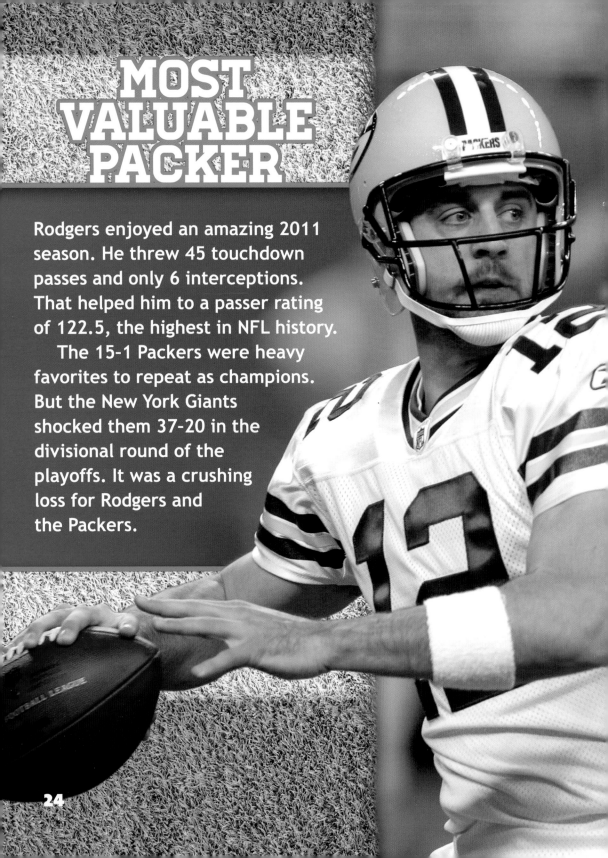

MOST VALUABLE PACKER

Rodgers enjoyed an amazing 2011 season. He threw 45 touchdown passes and only 6 interceptions. That helped him to a passer rating of 122.5, the highest in NFL history.

The 15-1 Packers were heavy favorites to repeat as champions. But the New York Giants shocked them 37-20 in the divisional round of the playoffs. It was a crushing loss for Rodgers and the Packers.

Rodgers drops back to pass in a 2011 game against the Detroit Lions.

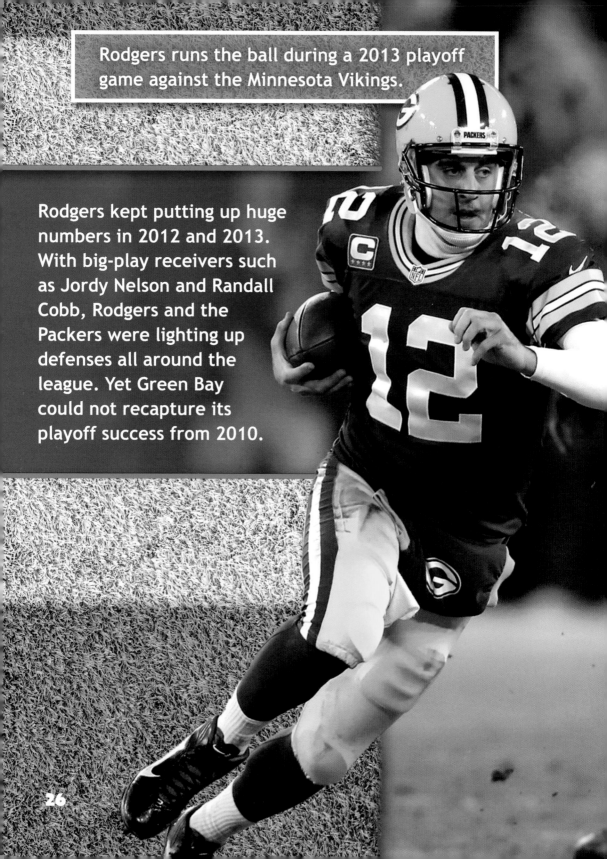

Rodgers runs the ball during a 2013 playoff game against the Minnesota Vikings.

Rodgers kept putting up huge numbers in 2012 and 2013. With big-play receivers such as Jordy Nelson and Randall Cobb, Rodgers and the Packers were lighting up defenses all around the league. Yet Green Bay could not recapture its playoff success from 2010.

FAST FACT

The San Francisco 49ers, Rodgers's favorite team when he was growing up, knocked Green Bay out of the playoffs after the 2012 and 2013 seasons.

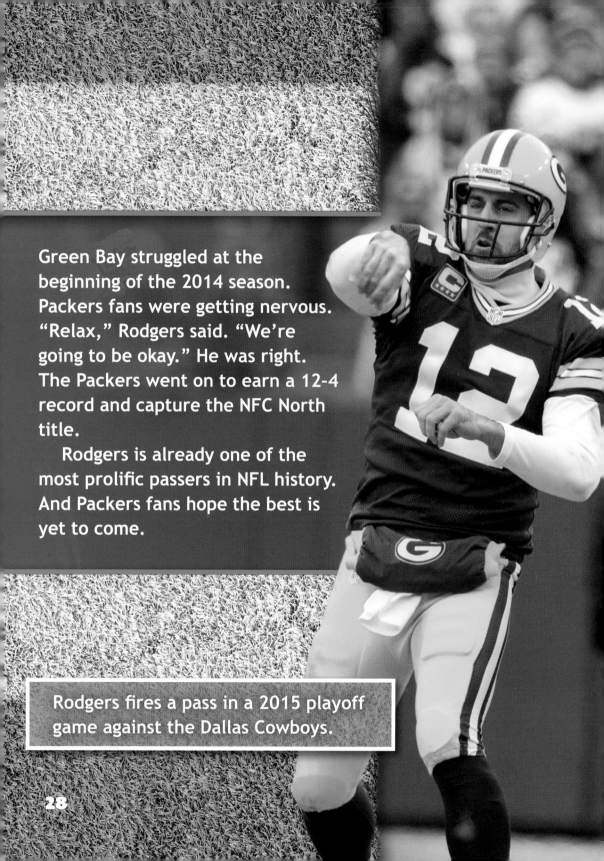

Green Bay struggled at the beginning of the 2014 season. Packers fans were getting nervous. "Relax," Rodgers said. "We're going to be okay." He was right. The Packers went on to earn a 12-4 record and capture the NFC North title.

Rodgers is already one of the most prolific passers in NFL history. And Packers fans hope the best is yet to come.

Rodgers fires a pass in a 2015 playoff game against the Dallas Cowboys.

FAST FACT
In the 2014 season, Rodgers won his second MVP award and led the Packers to the NFC Championship Game.

TIMELINE

1983
Aaron Rodgers is born on December 2 in Chico, California.

2002
Rodgers graduates from Pleasant Valley High School and attends nearby Butte Community College.

2003
Rodgers becomes a starter in his first season at the University of California.

2005
The Green Bay Packers select Rodgers with the twenty-fourth pick of the NFL Draft.

2008
Rodgers takes over as the starting quarterback for the Packers.

2011
On February 6, Rodgers leads the Packers to a Super Bowl victory over the Pittsburgh Steelers and is named Super Bowl MVP.

2011
Rodgers is named the 2011 NFL MVP.

2014
Rodgers leads Green Bay to a fourth straight NFC North title and wins his second NFL MVP award.

GLOSSARY

DIVISION I
The highest level of collegiate athletics.

PASSER RATING
A statistic that measures a quarterback's overall effectiveness on a scale from 0 to 158.3.

PROLIFIC
Producing in large numbers.

RIVAL
An opponent with which a team has a fierce and ongoing competition.

SCHOLARSHIP
Money given to a student to pay for education expenses.

SCOUT
To look for talented young players.

SEMI-PRO
A level of sports competition in which players are paid a very small amount to participate.

WILD-CARD
A team that makes the playoffs even though it did not win its division.

INDEX

ABOUT THE AUTHOR

Matt Scheff is an artist and author living in Alaska. He enjoys mountain climbing, deep-sea fishing, and curling up with his two Siberian huskies to watch football.